20 Answers

❧

Miracles

Karlo Broussard

Catholic
Answers
Press

20 Answers: Miracles
Karlo Broussard
© 2016 Catholic Answers

Published by Catholic Answers, Inc.
2020 Gillespie Way
El Cajon, California 92020
1-888-291-8000 orders
619-387-0042 fax
catholic.com

Printed in the United States of America

978-1-68357-014-1
978-1-68357-015-8 Kindle
978-1-68357-016-5 ePub

Introduction

If there's one thing that believers and non-believers can agree on, it's the problem of God's hiddenness. Which one of us has never cried out, "Where are you God? Show yourself!" Although it is true God doesn't overwhelm us with his presence, he does at times show himself through the gift of *miracles*. From Moses to Jesus, and throughout the history of the Church, God has been manifesting himself through wondrous deeds.

God desires that all men be saved and come to the knowledge of the truth (2 Tim. 1:5). This desire explains his choice to reveal himself as well as to perform miracles in order to confirm that revelation. Through miracles, God reminds us that he is present, and that there is more to the world than what meets the eye. They are powerful tools for leading unbelievers to the fullness of truth in the Catholic Church, and for strengthening the Faith in each of our hearts.

1. What is a miracle?

A *miracle* is an extraordinary sensible effect wrought by God that surpasses the power and order of created nature. That definition is a mouthful, so let's unpack it.

First, a miracle is an effect that is *beyond the power of created nature*. This excludes any sort of occurrence that may have unknown created causes—be it a force of nature, human activity, or pure spirits (angels or demons) acting only with their natural powers. Such effects might be wonderful and marvelous, but are not miracles.

An effect can be beyond created powers in three ways. First, a miracle may surpass created powers in the very nature of the effect produced. An example of this is the glorification of the resurrected body at the end of time. Such glorification is by its nature beyond the power of any created cause.

Second, the miraculous effect may surpass created powers with regard to the *subject* in which it is produced. For example, nature produces life in humans, but it cannot do so in a corpse. It is within the power of nature for a person to have sight, but nature cannot provide sight for one who is incurably blind. Notice how in these examples the miraculous is not identified in the *nature* of the effect—life and sight—but in the *subject*—a corpse and damaged eyes.

The third way a miracle may surpass created powers is according to the mode or manner in which the miraculous effect is produced. In other words, God may cause an effect that nature also produces, but beyond the way nature produces it. For example, a broken bone naturally mends itself over time, but if by someone's prayer the bone heals immediately, then it is miracle. Nature sometimes produces rain, but we consider it a miracle if rain falls by the command of a prophet.

So, a miracle must be the work of God, beyond all created *powers*. But not every work of God is a miracle. For example, God created the whole universe and each human soul, but these acts are not beyond the *order* of created nature. This is the next part of our definition of a miracle.

The third part is that it must be *extraordinary*. By this we mean it is outside the normal course of things, both natural and supernatural. To return to our example of the creation of the human soul: it is not extraordinary because God has decreed that human beings having souls is part of the ordinary course of things— that which completes our human nature. Likewise, the infusion of grace in the soul through the sacraments is not a miracle because God wills it as a regular occurrence in the supernatural order.

The last requirement for a miracle is that it be *sensible*—something that can be seen, heard, touched, felt, or smelled. This follows from the purpose of miracles, which we will look at next.

2. Why does God work miracles?

Many theologians have argued that given God's desire for all men to know him and be saved (2 Tim. 2:5), it is necessary that he reveal himself. But if God is to reveal himself, and moreover if he is to make belief in what he reveals a condition for our salvation, then his revelation must be authenticated. We must be able to discern if what appears to be a revelation is actually from God. That's what miracles are for.

This is also how Jesus understands his miracles, which the Gospels also call works or signs. "If I am not doing the works of my Father, then do not believe me," he said, "but if I do them, even though you do not believe me, believe the works" (John 10:37–38).

Notice that Jesus implicitly acknowledges the difficulty of believing his claim to divinity. This is something we all may struggle with sometimes. But Jesus reminds us to look to his miracles as rational justification for believing in his claims.

In keeping with Jesus' teaching, the First Vatican Council infallibly defined the purpose of miracles:

Nevertheless, in order that the submission of our faith should be in accordance with reason, it was God's will that there should be linked to the internal assistance of the Holy Spirit external indications of his revelation, that is to say divine acts, and first and foremost miracles and prophecies, which clearly demonstrating as they do the omnipotence and infinite knowledge of God, are the *most certain signs of revelation* and are suited to the understanding of all.[1]

The council fathers make clear that miracles are

meant to prove the authenticity of God's revelation, to make its divine character plain to see.

A second reason God performs miracles is to remind the human race that he exists. Although we can come to know that God exists through the observation of nature (Rom. 1:20), we often misinterpret nature's testimony. For example, in some ages and cultures mankind looked at nature and ended up with pantheism—a philosophical system that identifies God with the created world. In our time many more come away from their observation of nature believing that only matter exists and the world is merely a chance product of random jostling of molecules—a worldview known as materialism.

So, God makes his presence known through miracles to wake people up—to let us know that he exists and that he matters. One could say miracles are meant to break man from the spell of his senses so that he can better direct himself to his ultimate end, namely God.

Another reason why God performs miracles is to authenticate the claims of his Church. This would parallel the purpose of Jesus' miracles mentioned above. Just as Jesus' miracles give reason to believe his claims to divinity, so too can miracles in the Catholic Church give reason to believe its claims to have divine authority. The Catholic Church can say with Jesus, "If you don't believe what I say, believe my works."

Finally, God's miracles in the New Testament are theological signs—visible pointers to divine mysteries.

For example, St. John refers to Jesus' miracle at the Wedding in Cana as "the first of his signs" (John 2:11). But what is it a sign of?

One possible answer is it's a sign of the Messiah and the messianic age. Consider how the prophet Amos used the image of mountains dripping with sweet wine when prophesying about the restoration of David's kingdom (Amos 9:13).

With this prophecy as a backdrop, we can see why Jesus chose for his first miracle the changing of water into wine: to signify that he's the Messiah and the messianic age is upon them. That miracle was not just an authentication of Jesus' revelation about himself; it was an indication that something momentous was occurring in salvation history.

The bottom line is that miracles testify to God's love for humanity. He loves us too much to let us forget about him. He wants us to know that he has revealed himself to us so we can enter into a relationship with him and experience the happiness he desires us to have.

3. Are miracles too rare to believe in?

Modern skeptics argue that no reasonable man should believe in miracles. They take their cue from the eighteenth-century Scottish philosopher David Hume,[2] who asserted that it's irrational to believe in miracles because they are rare and contradict our uniform experience. Like Hume, skeptics base their argument on what some have called the "repeatability principle"— evidence for what occurs over and over (the regular) always outweighs evidence that does not (the rare).

But although it is true that a reasonable man should base his belief on the weight of evidence, it is not true that evidence for the regular always outweighs evidence for the rare.

If the repeatability principle were correct, then we would have to deny many things we hold as true. For example, the Big Bang was a singular event that does not repeat in our experience. Have you experienced any Big Bangs lately? I would guess the answer is no. I would also venture to say you have not watched anybody walk on the moon lately—or ever.

Now, if we held to Hume's principle, it would be irrational to believe the scientific account of the Big Bang and the historical fact that Neil Armstrong walked on the moon since these occurrences contradict our uniform experience. But the Big Bang is one of the most rigorously established theories in all of science, and all who are not conspiracy theorists believe Neil Armstrong's walk on the moon is a historical fact. The bottom line is that if we base our beliefs on what usually happens given our background knowledge, then we will cut ourselves off from a whole lot of truth.

Moreover, Hume's principle nullifies science itself. Science presupposes the possibility of discovering new things that may contradict uniform experience. Scientific laws are revised all the time based on new evidence. But according to the repeatability principle, scientists would never have good grounds to consider the contrary evidence in the first place; thus ruling out revision of scientific laws altogether. But to hold to such a position would negate all intellectual credibility.

A third reason why Hume's argument from uniform experience fails is because it begs the question. According to Hume's view, every miracle is disqualified from the start because every miracle is a rare event. But rarity is the essence of a miracle. A miracle, by definition, is an unusual event—something contrary to the ordinary course of things. So, Hume, and skeptics that follow suit, cannot reasonably reject a miracle because of its rarity.

Hume's argument also fails because it confuses *adding* evidence with *weighing* evidence. Consider the resurrection of Jesus. Hume's principle stipulates that we simply add up the evidence of all occasions where people died and did not rise and use it to overwhelm the claim that Jesus rose. But all this shows is people normally stay dead when they die and thus that resurrection is improbable. This is not a point of contention. Someone rising from the dead *is* highly improbable.

What Hume, and skeptics like him, seems to overlook is that a reasonable person does not base his beliefs merely on odds but on facts. So, the question must be, "Is there sufficient evidence to justify rational belief in Jesus' resurrection?" If the evidence were trustworthy, then belief in Jesus' resurrection would be reasonable even though resurrections are highly improbable. The same line of reasoning applies to any other alleged miracle.

So, although the rarity of miracles may be a reason for critical investigation, that doesn't mean it's unreasonable to believe in them.

4. Didn't the early Christians believe in miracles because they were part of a pre-scientific culture?

Many skeptics assert the only reason the early Christians believed in miracles was because they were part of a primitive culture where people were ignorant of the course of nature. People ignorant of science would perceive *any* strange natural phenomenon as a miracle.

There are three ways to respond to this claim. First, we should not overstate the alleged ignorance of people from past eras. When St. Joseph decided to divorce Mary quietly (Matt. 1:19) when he found out she was pregnant suggests he knew the laws of nature concerning the conception of children. He knew just as well as any modern gynecologist that in the ordinary course of nature women do not have babies without sexual relations with a man.

It is only after the angel appears to him and tells him the baby was miraculously conceived by the Holy

Spirit that he changes his mind. It wasn't his ignorance of science that led to his belief in the miracle. He knew very well that it is beyond the course of nature for a virgin to have a child. Joseph would not have been able to recognize that miracle unless he had a basic understanding of reproductive biology. This leads to our second response: the early Christians' testimony about miracles necessarily implies they understood the laws of nature. How could they recognize that something is a miracle, an extraordinary event, unless they first knew what was ordinary?

The Gospels speak of the audiences responding with fear and awe to Jesus' marvelous deeds (Mark 6:2, 51; 7:37; Luke 5:26; 7:16). Why would they do this unless they were able to recognize that such deeds were contrary to the ordinary course of nature? C.S. Lewis notes:

> If they were not known to be contrary to the laws of nature how could they suggest the presence of the supernatural? How could they be surprising unless they were seen to be exceptions to the rules? And how can anything be seen to be an exception till the rules are known?[3]

The healthy doubt of the miraculous embedded in the Gospel narratives is a third example that proves the early Christians did not accept miracles just because they were pre-scientific. Take for example St.

Luke's narrative of Zechariah's encounter with the angel (Luke 1:18). Zechariah, who was a priest and thus a religious man, refuses to believe the angel's announcement that his wife, Elizabeth, would conceive a son.

Why such doubt? Because Elizabeth was beyond childbearing years and Zechariah knew it. Far from being credulous because he was pre-scientific, he was initially a skeptic. Luke here makes it evident that first-century Jews were not so naive or ignorant that they were prepared to believe any sort of miraculous claim.

Luke's narrative of the Resurrection serves as another example. The first people to oppose the Christian message of the Resurrection were not atheists but the Sadducean high priests (see Acts 4:1–24). They were God-fearing Jews and the religious leaders of the day—and the biggest doubters of Jesus' resurrection.

We also see doubt concerning the Resurrection in the other Gospels. For example, Mark explains how the apostles doubted the Resurrection on two different occasions (see Mark 16:9–13). According to Matthew, some of the apostles doubted when Jesus appeared on the mountain in Galilee right before his ascension (Matt. 28:16–17). Finally, St. John records how Thomas doubted and would not believe unless he saw the risen Christ: "Unless I see in his hands the print of the nails, and place my finger in the mark of the nails, and place my hand in his side, I will not believe" (John 20:25).

Contrary to the skeptic's assumption, the people of Jesus' day were far from ignorant of the ordinary course of nature. They depended on their knowledge of nature to recognize real miracles when they saw them. And they treated reports of miracles with a fair amount of skepticism. The idea that early Christians believed miracles simply because they were pre-scientific is unfounded.

5. Are miracles incompatible with science?

Some skeptics argue that miracles are impossible because they violate the laws of nature. How are we to respond to such an objection? First, in order to understand whether miracles violate the laws of nature it's necessary to understand what laws of nature *are*.

Laws of nature are not mere descriptions of repeated events where one things follows another (e.g., when A, then B). The laws of nature describe what things are capable of producing given the powers they have by nature.

So, for example, the law of nature that tells us water freezes at thirty-two degrees Fahrenheit is simply a description of the nature of water having a tendency or disposition to freeze at that temperature. The law of nature that tells us fire burns is a description of the inherent power fire possesses.

The laws of nature, therefore, describe laws of *natures*—essences with inherent properties that manifest themselves when certain conditions are met. One could say the phrase "laws of nature" is shorthand for speaking about causal powers inherent in things.

It is this understanding that allows us to see how miracles are not really violations of the laws of nature (that is, proving them to be false). Instead, miracles are extraordinary sensible effects that *surpass* the power and causal order of created nature—because their cause is God.

For example, the natural forces in a human body cannot cause it to return to living health after it has died. But God can produce such an effect by directly giving life to a dead body. When he does this, as he did in the case of Jesus, it does not disprove the law of nature that states dead bodies stay dead. It remains true that dead bodies have no inherent power to come back to life. But God's supernatural power surpasses the body's natural powers.

Likewise, God can also *suspend* an inherent natural power without disproving a law of nature. Consider the miracle involving Shadrach, Meshach, and Abednego in Daniel 3. The intense fire into which they were thrown did not burn them. Did this disprove the law of nature that states fire burns? No. God simply willed that the inherent power of fire not manifest itself in that particular situation.

God has the power not only to surpass or suspend inherent natural powers but also to give an object a power it doesn't have by nature. Jesus' miracle of walking on water is an example of this (Matt. 14:22–23). Water in its liquid form does not have power within its nature to allow a human being to walk on it. But Jesus, being God, can give water such a property in a particular circumstance. This doesn't disprove the law of nature that states you will sink if you try to walk on water, which you can easily prove for yourself in the nearest lake or pool.

So miracles do not violate the natural order—they are not contrary to nature but above or beyond nature.

Skeptics often pit miracles and science against each other, claiming you have to choose one or the other. But this is a false dichotomy. You can accept both if you acknowledge the existence of an all-powerful God. So, miracles aren't the real problem for the skeptic—God is.

6. Do miracles in non-Christian religions undermine the truth of Christianity?

Skeptics argue Christians cannot use miracles to validate Christianity's claims to truth because other religions, which contradict Christianity, have miraculous validation of their claims. So, either Christianity is false and these other religions are true, or miracles are just something every culture and religion invents.

How do we respond?

First, not every account of the miraculous in other religions is historically reliable—often because they were not recorded until long after they were supposed to have happened. For example, the story about the Buddha flying and shooting sparks from *Mahāvastu*, a text compiled between the second century B.C. and fourth century A.D., many centuries after the Buddha's life.[4] Compare that to the written records of Jesus' miracles, which in some cases date only twenty-five years after the events and were written by people who claimed to see the events.

Other qualities render miraculous accounts unreliable. Consider how Philostratus, a second- and third-century Athenian sophist, narrates Apollonius, a first-century Greek philosopher and so-called miracle worker, speaking at length with the kings of Babylon and Nineveh when those places were ancient ruins long before that time.

Second, even if the account of a marvelous deed is historically reliable, it may not be a miracle worked by God. It may be a trick or an illusion of the kind you might see at a magic show. It might be a *supernormal* event—something not beyond nature but beyond the normal. For example, it is known some yogis have extraordinary abilities to control their bodily functions, such as lowering their heart rate to endure extreme temperatures or going long periods without food. Such feats, however rare, are not beyond the natural powers of man and so are not miracles.

A marvelous event might also be the effect of a being that transcends the visible order of nature: namely an angel or demon. Such an event would seem supernatural to humans since it transcends the order of nature we observe with our senses, but it would not transcend the *created* order since demonic beings are created beings. So it, too, would be a supernormal event.

None of these reported marvels—those that are fictitious or historically unreliable, those that have natural explanations, and those that are caused by angels or demons—are actually miracles, and so do not undermine the evidential value Christian miracles have for Christianity.

Now, what if God were the cause of a miracle in a non-Christian religion? Would that disprove Christianity's claims?

It seems reasonable to say that God could choose to perform a miracle for a non-Christian, or even in a non-Christian religious setting, without validating that religion's beliefs. For example, we can imagine God healing the sick son of a Hindu mother, even through the actions of a Hindu holy man or ceremony, simply to reaffirm for her the reality of the transcendent, or because he has an important plan for that child in the future.

A miracle claim in a non-Christian religion would only count as evidence against a proposition in Christianity if the miracle were unquestionably evidence for a contradictory religious assertion. For example, Jesus' cure of the paralytic in Mark 2:10–12 validated his claim to have power to forgive sins. A truly contradictory miracle claim in a non-Christian religion would assert that Jesus did not have that power, or that the authority for it rests with someone else.

But even if such a claim presented itself, the evidence for Jesus' miracles in confirmation of his teachings is so sound that we should be instantly skeptical of wondrous deeds that support doctrines contrary to Christianity. Chances are they're human tricks, natural marvels, or lies from the devil.

7. Since they deal with faith and the supernatural, isn't it impossible to investigate miracles as historical events?

Some skeptics argue that since miracles deal with the power of God and supernatural events, they can't be the subject of historical research. Therefore, we can never say that miracles can be known as historical facts.

There are two major problems with this kind of objection. First, for every alleged supernatural miracle there will be circumstantial details surrounding the reported event that are not supernatural, and therefore fall within anyone's boundaries of historical study.

Take the resurrection of Jesus, for example. The early Christians report his tomb was empty and that they saw Jesus. These reports are subject to historical verification. In this case the empty tomb is attested to by six different sources.

- Paul's preaching in 1 Corinthians 15:1–3 is one. He preaches that Jesus was buried and raised, which implies the tomb was empty.

- Scholars argue that Mark's account of the empty tomb is part of the source material he used for his Gospel, which dates all the way back to A.D. 37— only seven years after the actual event (another reason why it's considered historically reliable).[5]

- Matthew's account of the empty tomb comes from a different source as well because he records things the others do not: the guard at the tomb and the narrative of the Jews conspiring to fabricate a story that the apostles stole the body.

- Luke's account reveals he used an independent source. He narrates how the two disciples went to the tomb to verify the women's claim that the tomb was empty. He didn't get this from Mark because Mark doesn't record it and as all scholars agree the synoptic Gospels (Matthew, Mark, and Luke) are independent of John.

- Because John's account of the empty tomb is independent, he is a fifth source.

- Finally, Luke's record of Peter's first sermon on the Resurrection in Acts 2 comes from an independent source. Peter's message about David prophesying the resurrection of the Christ is unique (Acts

2:25–32), thus indicating its independence from the source material for the four Gospels and Paul.

Since multiple attestation is a key indicator for historical reliability, we can confidently judge, as a matter of historical inquiry, that Jesus' tomb was empty as the New Testament records. This is an important circumstantial detail surrounding the miracle.

Along with the empty tomb, historians can also evaluate the historical reliability of the alleged resurrected appearances. For example, Jesus' appearance to Mary Magdalene and the women is multiply attested to by Mark (Mark 16:9), John (John 20:11–18), and Matthew (Matt. 28:8–10).

The report of Jesus' appearance to women also satisfies what historians call the "embarrassment criterion": the more embarrassing a detail is, the more likely it's a historical fact. In the world of first-century Judaism, the testimony of women was not held in high esteem.[6] This being the case, it would be an embarrassment to suggest women were the first witnesses of the resurrected Jesus. Why would the apostles record such a detail unless it was true?

Jesus' appearance to Peter by himself is historically reliable because both Luke (Luke 24:34) and Paul (1 Cor. 15:5) testify to it; thus satisfying the multiple attestation criterion. We also learn from different sources that Jesus appeared to "the twelve." Paul, Luke, and John record the immediate appearance after the Resurrection (1 Cor. 15:5; Luke 24:36–43; John 20:19–20), John records Jesus' later appearance on the seashore (John 21), and Matthew records Jesus' final appearance to the twelve before the Ascension (Matt. 28:19–20).

Paul tells us in 1 Corinthians 15:6 that Jesus appeared to 500 brethren at once. He also records that Jesus appeared to James, which we can evaluate historically in light of Paul's conversation with James when he traveled to Jerusalem, according to Galatians 1:19. Finally, Jesus' appearance to "all the apostles" is affirmed by three independent sources—Paul (1 Cor. 15:7), Luke's Gospel source (Luke 24:50–51), and Luke's source for Acts (Acts 1:2, 6–11).

And so we see, taking the example of one of the central Christian miracles, that miraculous events are not beyond the boundaries of historical investigation. By using legitimate historical criteria—such as multiple attestation and embarrassment—historians are able to investigate and gauge the historical reliability of circumstantial facts that surround miraculous events without the need for faith or for considering the supernatural agency responsible for the event.

Now, it's important to note that historical investigation does not entirely preclude inquiry into a supernatural cause for the reported event. This is the second problem with the objection.

There is a sense in which supernatural agency does

enter into historical investigation. For example, once the circumstantial details are established as credible, the historian must face the question, "What is the most probable *explanation* for them?" Such a question does fall within the parameters of historical study.

With regard to the resurrection of Jesus, the historian must ask if the resurrection hypothesis or some alternative natural explanation best explains the circumstantial details. If no explanation can account for the facts as well as the miraculous explanation, then the historian is justified in considering it as the best *historical* explanation.

We will address the strength of the literal resurrection hypothesis in comparison to alternative explanations in answer 10.

8. Did the fantastic miracles in the Old Testament actually happen?

Before even considering this question it is important to note that it's not a deal breaker when it comes to the truth of God's existence or the truth of Jesus' resurrection from the dead. If God exists, and he has revealed himself through Jesus, then Christianity is true, and the rest is merely "in-house" concerns—questions that Christians ask and debate among themselves. The historical reliability of miracles in the Old Testament doesn't have to be an obstacle to faith in Christ.

With that said, let's address the skepticism that often surrounds Old Testament miracles. If someone doubts the Old Testament accounts of miracles just because he thinks miracles are too fantastical, like the splitting of the Red Sea (Exod. 14:21), then his issue is not historical but philosophical. If, however, the problem is a historical issue, like whether there was a global flood, then there are two major questions that must be addressed.

The first is, "Are the narratives intended to be literal accounts in the first place?" For example, the Church allows for the creation story to be interpreted as a figurative story meant to convey certain underlying historical truths about God, man, and the universe.[7] The literary style of the first few chapters of the book of Genesis suggests that it may not have been written as a strictly literal account. Are the Old Testament miracle narratives like this?

On this point the Church allows some room for discussion. For example, with regard to miracles the First Vatican Council only mentioned the miracles of "both Moses and the prophets" and "Christ the Lord himself" as evidence for God's revelation.[8] It didn't specify which *particular* miracles. The only specific Bible miracles that must be accepted with divine faith are the miracles mentioned in the Creed—Christ's virginal conception and birth, and his resurrection from the dead. Then there are biblical miracles that the Church affirms as historical, such as the miracle at the wedding of Cana and the miracle of the loaves (CCC 1335); these require religious assent.

Such freedom for discussion was given explicit approval by Pope Pius XII in his 1943 encyclical *Divino Afflante Spiritu*[9], where he acknowledged the presence of various literary forms in the Bible. This approach allowed biblical scholars to argue, for example, the story of Jonah was not historical but a parable of some sort. Even the book of Tobit is seen by some to not be history but pious romance.[10]

Now, even though there is *permission* for diverse interpretations for particular miracle stories in both the Old and New Testaments, that doesn't mean a non-literal interpretation of a specific event (or events) is always the best. For example, the whole history of Israel's exodus from Egypt and settlement in Canaan is bound up with the miracles narrated. To deny the reality of the miracles involved in the exodus narrative would be to deny the foundation of Israel's history.[11] This calls for stricter interpretative license than one would have with the story of Jonah.

Furthermore, using the various criteria of historiography (study of historical writings), scholars have compellingly argued that many miracles of both the Old and New Testaments are literal and historically reliable.[12]

The second major question is, "If the miracle accounts are meant to be taken literally, how much did natural causes and powers contribute to the miraculous events?" In other words, might the narratives have been describing literal but non-miraculous events? For example, it seems natural forces did play some role in the event of the Israelites' passage through the Red Sea: "[T]he Lord drove the sea back by a strong east wind all night, and made the sea dry land" (Exod. 14:21). It's even possible natural phenomena played some part in many of the plagues of Egypt.

But the involvement of natural phenomena does not necessarily make an event non-miraculous. It might simply relocate where the miracle lay. Rather than lying in a bizarre event otherwise unknown, it would lie in Moses' actions to evoke natural calamities at will. Other events subject to the same interpretative principle include the crossing of the Jordan River and the tumbling walls of Jericho.[13] Just because natural causes were involved, God's divine power is no less evident.

The idea that natural causes could have been used by God in Old Testament miracles fits with the third (and lowest) category of miracles we saw in answer 1, in which God may cause an effect that nature usually produces, but beyond the way nature produces it. The natural explanations mentioned above fit the bill. The drying up of the sea at certain parts and the death of Egyptian children may be natural phenomena, but if done by the command of Moses with God's power, then they constitute a miracle of the third degree.

So, we have some room to play when it comes to interpreting particular miraculous events in the Old Testament. But what the Church does not permit is the denial of the miraculous in its entirety, especially the miracles of Moses, the prophets, and Jesus. God has revealed himself and provided external helps, namely miracles, to verify that revelation and provide a reasonable basis for faith.

9. Are the miracles of Jesus historically reliable?

There are two ways to approach the historicity of Jesus' miracles: a *general* way and a *specific* way. The *specific* assessment, which includes looking at each miracle in light of the criteria for historicity (clues that indicate an event or saying is historically reliable), is far too detailed for this booklet.[14] So we will discuss the general way.

It's helpful to note first that the Gospel writers record things about Jesus' miraculous deeds that are not beneficial for persuading people to believe. For example, Mark records the accusation that Jesus performs his exorcisms by the power of the devil: "He is possessed by Be-elzebul, and by the prince of demons he casts out the demons" (Mark 3:22). It's more probable than not that the scribes really did make this accusation because it doesn't make sense for Mark (or the other evangelists) to make something up that could undermine the reputation of Jesus.[15]

Now, if that's evidence that the accusation is historical (remember the "embarrassment criterion"), then it's reasonable to conclude that Jesus' contemporaries regarded him as a man with remarkable powers who performed remarkable deeds. Why else would they make such a charge? It is hard to see why Jesus' toughest critics would acknowledge him as having supernatural power unless there was wide agreement that he was performing exorcisms.

Another point to keep in mind is that the style of Jesus' miracles was far different from the first-century milieu of wonder-workers, which for historians suggests that the wonders he performed were historical and not part of a local myth tradition. In his book, *An Introduction to New Testament Christology*, Bible scholar Raymond Brown identifies five unique characteristics of Jesus' miracles compared with those found in ancient Greek and Jewish stories. We'll look at two of them here.

One is that Jesus performs miracles by his own authority. If you read the Gospels carefully, Jesus doesn't say things like, "*In the name of God*, rise and walk" but simply "Rise, take up your pallet and walk" (Mark 2:9). When he raises Jairus's daughter from the dead, he says, "Little girl, *I say* to you, arise."

This is unlike Old Testament prophets such as Elijah and Elisha, who call on the power of God in order to raise the dead (see 1 Kings 17:17–22; 2 Kings 4:32–35). We find a similar style of miracle working—whether through magical formulas, paraphernalia, or prayers to the gods—among Greek and Roman sources.[16] Jesus stands apart by working wonders through his own power.

A second characteristic that is unique to Jesus is that he doesn't perform miracles for the sake of showing off. Where other ancient wonder-workers of that era aimed to astonish and solicit admiration,[17] Jesus shied away from drawing attention to himself.

For example, when Herod asks Jesus to perform a miracle to show off his power, Jesus refuses to do so (Luke 23:8–12). Jesus was frustrated by the Pharisees' constant requests for a sign (Mark 8:11–12). Even Satan tries to get Jesus to show off his power but Jesus refuses (Matt. 4:5–7).

Furthermore, when Jesus did perform his miracles, he did so in a way that drew attention away from himself. This is evident in his command that the healed leper remain silent: "See that you say nothing to any one; but go, show yourself to the priest" (Mark 1:44). In many other places in Scripture, Jesus can be seen admonishing others not to publicize his identity or his works.

It is also reasonable to accept Jesus' miracles as history because of how restrained the Gospel narratives are in describing them. These accounts are starkly different from the frivolous and exaggerated elements found in the fraudulent Gnostic Gospels that appeared in the early centuries of the Church.

Take, for example, Mark's account of the Resurrection. It is simple and unembellished—he doesn't even describe Jesus' rising. You would think that if he were making it up he would have embellished it to make it sell. Why not include extraordinary details like those found in the apocryphal Gospel of Peter—giant angels, a talking cross, a voice from heaven, and Jesus coming out of the tomb as a gigantic figure whose head reaches to the clouds?

Or contrast the simplicity of the miracle narratives in the Gospels with that in another Gnostic text, the *Infancy Gospel of Thomas,* which depicts the child Jesus making clay sparrows fly and twice cursing other children to death—one for spilling water and one for bumping into Jesus on the street.

It is amazing to think the Gospel writers did not give in to the temptation to exaggerate Jesus' miracles, to make them more dramatic and appealing to potential converts. Their restraint, along with Jesus' unique style and the testimony of his enemies, are all evidence for the historical reliability of the accounts of Jesus' miracles.

10. Was Jesus' resurrection a real historical event?

Like any historical investigation, the inquiry into the historicity of Jesus' resurrection seeks to determine if it is the best explanation of certain historical facts. The historical facts recorded in the Gospels that need to be explained include:

- Jesus' tomb was discovered empty.

- Women were the first to see the empty tomb and the resurrected Jesus.

- Jesus appeared to different people on different occasions in bodily and glorious[18] form.

- Jesus' resurrection was central to the early Christians' belief and was something worth dying for.

- The early Christians didn't find another Messiah to follow but continued professing Jesus as Savior and Lord after his death.

If the competing natural hypotheses fail in accounting for the above facts, while the resurrection hypothesis succeeds, then we're justified in accepting Jesus' resurrection as a historical fact.[19]

Take, for example, the most popular competing theory, the Conspiracy Theory. This theory suggests the early Christians stole Jesus' body and lied together (conspired) about the resurrected appearances. This theory explains the empty tomb, the post-mortem appearances, and even the Christian claim that Jesus was Lord; however, it doesn't adequately explain why the Gospel writers record women as the first witnesses of the empty tomb and the resurrected Jesus. As we saw earlier, women's testimony was not held in high esteem in first-century Judaism[20] and the Gospel-writing conspirators just as easily could have chosen men to be the first witnesses—perhaps Joseph of Arimathea and Nicodemus—to make their story more credible.

Furthermore, the Conspiracy Theory doesn't fit with the early Christian belief in a resurrected *Messiah*. Why would the conspirators make this up when a resurrected Messiah was not even a hope for first-century Jews?[21] First-century Jews were not expecting *anyone* to rise before the end of time.[22] This is not something that would persuade the Jews to join the new religion.

Finally, this theory fails to explain why the early Christians believed the Resurrection was worth dying for. It is unreasonable to think the early Christians would undergo harsh persecution and death for what they knew to be a lie.

Other alternative explanations appeal to early Christian subjective experiences to explain their belief in Jesus' resurrection. For example, the Hallucination Theory suggests the Christians simply imagined that they saw Jesus. The Vision Theory puts forward the idea that Jesus appeared to certain early Christians in visions, causing them to believe mistakenly that he had risen from the dead.

Although these explanations could possibly explain the alleged appearances of a resurrected Jesus, they fall short in accounting for the other facts. For example, they don't explain the empty tomb. If the Christians were merely hallucinating or having visions of Jesus, then the skeptics could have easily produced the body. Given that Jesus was so popular, and he was placed in a tomb that belonged to Joseph of Arimathea, a member of the Sanhedrin (a group of Jewish leaders), it's reasonable to conclude the location of Jesus' tomb would have been known.

Moreover, the subjective explanations might be adequate to explain a single appearance of Jesus, but it fails to explain the *multiple* appearances to different people on different occasions.

For example, we know Jesus appeared privately to Mary Magdalene (Mark 16:9), the women at the tomb (Luke 24:10), Peter (1 Cor. 15:5), and James (1 Cor. 15:7). He appeared to the twelve (1 Cor. 15:5) and did so on many different occasions—in the upper room on the night of the Resurrection (John 20:19–23), on the seashore (John 21), for a succession of forty days (Acts 1:3), and on the Mount of Olives before his ascension (Matt. 28:18–20). St. Paul writes that Jesus even appeared to 500 brethren at the same time, many of whom were still alive when Paul penned his letter (1 Cor. 15:6).

How can so many different people hallucinate the same thing or have the same vision (drawing from it the same erroneous conclusion) at different times and in different places? It doesn't make sense.

The bodily nature of the encounters with the resurrected Jesus is another problem for the Hallucination and Vision theories. For example, there were three times when the resurrected Jesus ate with his disciples—with his apostles on the seashore (John 21:14–15), in the home of the two disciples traveling on the road to Emmaus (Luke 24:28–30), and with the apostles in Jerusalem (Luke 24:41–43). Jesus even told the apostle Thomas to touch the wounds in his hands and side from his crucifixion (John 20:27). Hallucinations and visions don't eat food and can't be touched.

These subjective theories are also bankrupt when it comes to explaining the unique characteristics of Jesus' resurrection and the early Christian belief in Jesus as Lord. The existence of Jesus' resurrected, *glorified* body is not something that would have been present in the Christians' minds to project onto reality. The Jewish conception of resurrection was a return to the same kind of bodily life as before death.[23] Pagans at the time didn't even have a conception of a bodily resurrection.[24] For this reason, the Hallucination Theory fails.

Furthermore, visions of dead people were common in the first century. Such an occurrence would not give the Christians reason to think Jesus was risen from the dead, much less to continue professing their crucified leader as Messiah and Lord and making the Resurrection a central doctrine.

A final major alternative theory is the Swoon Theory, which says Jesus didn't die on the cross but merely fell unconscious (swooned) and later revived in the tomb, then walked out.

This alternative theory, too, fails as a reasonable explanation of the historical facts. First, because it doesn't adequately explain the detail it attempts to explain: namely the empty tomb. Is it reasonable to believe a half-dead Jesus, who had been tortured and nailed to a cross for hours before passing out, would have had enough strength to roll away the heavy stone covering the tomb? Is it credible to think Jesus would have been able to get past the guards stationed there, and make his way to safety unseen?

The Swoon Theory also fails to explain why the early Christians believed Jesus was raised in a glorified and incorruptible state. A half-dead man covered in blood is a far cry from the idea of a glorious victor over death that is Messiah and Lord.

In contrast to these alternative explanations, the glorious resurrection of Jesus succeeds in explaining *all* the facts. Obviously if Jesus rose from the dead, the tomb would be empty. His glorious resurrection would also explain the alleged postmortem appearances, the unique qualities of Jesus' resurrected body, and why they professed a resurrected Messiah. Finally, the resurrection hypothesis adequately explains how the early Christians could continue to profess Jesus as God despite the fact that he was crucified and died.

As with all historical events, it's impossible to have *absolute* certitude of the Resurrection based on the historical evidence. However, when one considers the historical details surrounding the accounts of Jesus' resurrection, and the fact that alternative explanations fail to explain these details, it is reasonable to conclude Jesus' resurrection was a historical event.

11. What sort of miracles did the apostles perform?

Before ascending into heaven, Jesus promised that the apostles would receive the Holy Spirit and be his witnesses to the ends of the earth (Acts 1:8). They would fulfill that mission in their preaching and ultimately by giving their lives in martyrdom. But they also gave witness to Jesus and his lordship through miracles.

The apostolic miracles can be divided into two broad categories: miracles proper and wondrous deeds. Miracles proper involve extraordinary occurrences that require divine power (see answer 1). Wondrous deeds, however, though beyond the ordinary, do not require divine power but merely *superhuman* power.

There are five types of miracles proper. The first is *resuscitations from the dead*, of which there are two narratives—Peter raises the disciple Tabitha (Acts 9:36–42) and Paul raises the young man Eutychus (Acts 20:9–12).

Exorcisms are the second type. One account is of a slave girl with soothsaying powers (Acts 16:16–18). Luke records how she constantly followed Paul and annoyingly cried out that he was a servant of God.

Paul discerned the presence of an evil spirit, rebuked it, and made it come out of her.

The exorcisms performed by the deacon Philip in Samaria are also recorded. After preaching to the Samaritans, he drove out the unclean spirits of those possessed and eventually baptized those who believed (Acts 8:6–8). We are also told that many unclean spirits were driven out of the possessed after Peter's shadow passed over them while in Jerusalem (Acts 5:15–16).

A third type of miracles proper is miraculous *cures*, which take on multiple forms. For example, there are accounts of healing the lame—Peter heals a lame man at the temple gate (Acts 3:1–16) and a paralytic in Aeneas (Acts 9:33–35), Paul heals the lame man of Lystra (Acts 14:7–9), and Philip heals the lame in Samaria (Acts 8:7).

There is also an account of healing the blind, in which Saul is on the receiving end. Ananias, a disciple, receives instruction from the Lord to visit Saul, lays hands on Saul, and restores Saul's vision (Acts 9:17–18).

The apostles healed diseases as well. For example, Paul cures Publius' father of dysentery (Acts 28:7–8) and heals a multitude of people plagued by disease on the island of Malta (Acts 28:9).

Healing not only came through the direct hand of Paul but also through his handkerchief (Acts 19:11–12)—an event that testifies to the early Christian veneration of relics. Even Peter's shadow became an instrument of healing for the sick when it passed over them (Acts 5:15).

The fourth type of miracles proper is the *punishment miracle*—an unpleasant occurrence that is miraculously wrought as a result of grave sin. There are two narratives of such miracles. The first is the death of Anania and Saphira, who are struck dead at Peter's feet for lying to the Holy Spirit (Acts 5:5–11). Although their death was not a direct action of Peter's, he was involved in denouncing their sin.

There is also a case of punishment by blindness that involves Paul and the sorcerer Elymas (Acts 13:9–12). After rebuking Elymas for his defilement in divining activities, Paul announces the hand of the Lord is upon him and that he would be blind for a time.

The fifth and final kind of miracle proper found in the Acts of the Apostles is the *suspension of spatial limitations*. After the deacon Philip baptized an Ethiopian eunuch, Luke records that Philip was caught up in the Spirit of the Lord and disappeared from the eunuch, finding himself in Azotas (Acts 8:39).

The other broad category of apostolic miracles is wondrous deeds and occurrences. Recall that these actions do not require divine power, but nevertheless are deeds that require some sort of superhuman power.

One such miracle is when the apostles were gathered together for the feast of Pentecost (Acts 2:2–6). They heard a sound like rushing wind and saw tongues of fire appearing on their heads. On that same day the apostles preached and people gathered from the various nations heard the apostles' message in their own languages (Acts 2:4–12). On another occasion the apostles' preaching caused a building they were gathered in to shake (Acts 4:31).

There are also accounts of the apostles miraculously being freed from captivity. For example, after being thrown into prison by the Sadducees, the apostles were able to escape because an angel opened the prison doors of their cell (Acts 5:17–25). The same happened for Peter when Herod threw him into prison (Acts 12:5–11). Paul and Silas experienced a similar occurrence; but for them the prison doors of their cell were opened due to an unusual earthquake (Acts 16:25–30) and they did not escape. The wondrous event led to the conversion of the jailer.

Finally, we're told the apostles performed many "signs and wonders" among the people in Jerusalem (Acts 2:43; 5:12) and among the Gentiles (Acts 15:12). Whether these were miracles proper we don't know and thus can only speculate.

The apostolic miracles and wondrous events witness to Jesus in as much as the apostles were preaching in the *name* of Jesus. The apostles and early Christians didn't perform miraculous deeds for the sake of impressing people. They did them to promote the message and identity of Jesus Christ. Even the wondrous occurrences they experienced were meant to enable the apostles to continue their apostolic preaching.

12. What role do miracles have in the Catholic Church?

There have been various kinds of miracles that make up the patrimony of the Catholic Church. One category of such miracles is *eucharistic miracles*. Catholics believe every time a priest prays the words of consecration over the bread and wine—"this is my body . . . this is my blood"—the substance of bread and wine (what it *is*) changes into Jesus' body, blood, soul, and divinity while the accidents of bread and wine (how it *appears*) remain. The remaining presence of the bread and wine's accidental properties is a miracle in its own right. But this is not what is normally called a eucharistic miracle.

A eucharistic miracle occurs when the accidents of bread and wine change into real human flesh and real human blood. There are numerous documented instances of such an occurrence in the history of the Church, and we'll look at some of them in greater depth later. A eucharistic miracle can also involve the unusual preservation of the accidental properties of bread and wine over long periods of time.

Saints' *incorruptible bodies* are another example of a miracle type we find in Catholic history. Such a miracle occurs when a saint's body, or a part of it, is preserved in a way that defies the normal process of decomposition. Unlike mummies, which have dry and hardened skin and bones, some of the saints' uncorrupted bodies retain soft skin and pliable limbs even centuries after their death. In another answer we look at some examples of this type of miracle, too.

Many of these *incorruptibles* have been found to give off sweet odors. Others, like St. Francis Xavier's body, have produced blood that defies any scientific explanation. Skeptics try to reduce the incorruptibles to the status of mummies, but the evidence overwhelmingly points beyond the natural.

Finally, in Catholic history there are scores of documented *healing* miracles. For example, there are the officially recognized miracles associated with the bathing waters of Lourdes, France (sixty-nine in total). There are also the healing miracles associated with canonized saints. A fairly recent example is the healing of Floribeth Moral Diaz of Costa Rica through the intercession of Pope St. John Paul II. With only a short time to live due to an inoperable brain aneurysm, she requested John Paul II's intercession and was healed. This provided the second miracle needed to advance his path to sainthood.

Historical miracles in the Catholic Church serve several purposes. First, they lend credibility to the claim that the Catholic Church is the original church founded by Jesus.

Second, these miracles move individuals to faith in a way that goes beyond internal experiences and private inspiration. Not everyone has powerful conversion experiences like St. Paul, who, after seeing the risen Jesus, converted to Christianity after several years of persecuting Christians. But by working miracles in history, God continues to give people reason to believe.

Finally, miracles point to the end of time when all of creation will be renewed. The healing miracles and incorruptibles focus our attention on the restoration of the body in the bodily resurrection, about which St. Paul writes, "What is sown is perishable, what is raised is imperishable" (1 Cor. 15:42). Eucharistic miracles remind us of God's sovereignty over physical reality and how he will transform the material world in the new heaven and new earth (CCC 1043–1047; Rev. 21:1).

Jesus did not rob us of the privilege to experience the wonder of his works. He continues to *wow* us with miracles in the Catholic Church in order that we may believe him and his Father who sent him.

13. What have been the most famous Catholic healing miracles?

Perhaps the most famous healing of recent times is that of Gemma di Giorgi, a Sicilian woman who was healed of her blindness at the age of seven by St. Pio of Pietrelcina—commonly known as Padre Pio.

Gemma was born on Christmas day in 1939, in the small town of Ribera, Sicily. Within the first three months of her life it became apparent to Gemma's parents there was something wrong with her eyesight. After she was examined by two doctors, it was discovered that Gemma had no pupils and she was declared blind. From a medical standpoint there was nothing that could be done. Without pupils, it's impossible to see.

At the age of seven, Gemma's grandmother decided to take her to visit Padre Pio in San Giovanni Rotondo in order to request his intercession for healing. Although there are differing accounts of the actual process of the healing—some say she partially regained sight on the train ride to San Giovanni and others say she received sight only in San Giovanni—there is no disagreement that Gemma received her sight as a result of St. Pio's intercession.

Fr. Charles Mortimer Carty describes how St. Pio called Gemma out of a crowd by name without any prior knowledge of who she was:

> They were both lost in the crowd . . . attending [Padre Pio's] Mass, when at the end while the silence was still intense, everyone heard a voice calling: "Gemma, come here!" The grandmother pushed her way to the altar. . . . [Padre Pio] smiled at Gemma and told her that she must make her First Communion. He heard her confession and then stroked her eyes with his hand.[25]

Although Gemma couldn't see right away, she would see later after a subsequent encounter with St. Pio. Fr. Carty explains:

Padre Pio saw them [Gemma and her grandmother] later and said: 'May the Madonna bless you, Gemma. Be a good girl!' At this moment the child gave a frantic cry, she could see.[26]

It has been seventy years since the miracle and Gemma can still see to this day. But what is perhaps most interesting is that her pupils were not miraculously restored in the healing—that is to say, her physical eye structure did not change. They still look like the eyes of a blind woman. From a medical and scientific perspective she should not be able to see, and doctors cannot explain how she can.[27]

Many other famous healings have been observed in the town of Lourdes, France, where a spring connected with a nineteenth-century apparition of the Blessed Virgin Mary draws hundreds of thousands of pilgrims every year. Of the more than 6,000 healings alleged to have occurred there, the Church has approved sixty-nine. (This is not to say that all the others were not real miracles, but that only sixty-nine have been investigated and met the stringent criterion the Church uses for investigating miracle claims.)

The two approved healing miracles that stand out

among the others are those of Marie Lebranchu and Marie Lemarchand—both of whom were healed of pulmonary tuberculosis (Koch's bacillus) on successive days in 1892. Both women had suffered from the disease for two years and had reached its terminal stages. Marie Lebranchu, thirty-five years old at the time, came to the baths weighing less than sixty pounds with bodily disfiguration. Marie Lemarchand, who was eighteen, approached the baths with deeply ulcerated areas on her face, caused by tuberculosis, that partly destroyed her nose and mouth.

After bathing in the miraculous waters, both women were healed of their tuberculosis immediately. Although it would take some time before Marie Lebranchu's body was restored, Marie Lemarchand's skin and face were miraculously restored the next day. Neither woman had a relapse of the disease. Marie Lebranchu lived in perfect health until she died in 1920 and Marie Lemarchand married and became the mother of eight children, living free from the disease until she died, long after her cure was declared miraculous, in 1908.

14. What is the miracle that made Fatima famous?

In 1917 in the town of Fatima, Portugal, three young Portuguese children claimed to experience repeated apparitions from a lady from heaven who spoke to them about the need for mankind to repent. In order to prove their visions authentic, the lady promised to perform a miracle on the thirteenth day of October. Talk of the miracle caused great distress and persecution for the three children, but nevertheless they stuck to their story.

On the day the miracle was promised to occur, roughly 70,000 people gathered to witness it. The crowd included not only peasants but also skeptical journalists, priests, academics, and even a distinguished eye specialist. They had no idea what type of miracle to expect. The only thing the children knew was that the miracle would occur around midday.

Not long after midday, after many hours of pouring rain drenched the crowd, the clouds parted and the sun began to shine. But it didn't shine in the usual way. It shined with different colors and was perceived to be spinning on its axis. As if this weren't enough, ten minutes later the crowd was terrified to see the sun appear to plunge toward the earth. Many thought it was the end of the world.

The sun then went back to its rightful place and the crowds realized their wet clothes were now dry. Fr. John de Marchi, a witness of the events, provides four credible witnesses for validation in his book *The True Story of Fatima*. The first is Almeida Garrett, a professor from Coimbra University in Portugal. Garrett describes the events as follows:

The sun, a few moments before, had broken through the thick layer of clouds which hid it, and shone clearly and intensely. . . . It was a remarkable fact that one could fix one's eyes on this brazier of light and heat without any pain in the eyes or blinding of the retina. . . . The sun's disc did not remain immobile. This was not the sparkling of a heavenly body, for it spun round on itself in a mad whirl. . . The sun, whirling wildly, seemed to loose itself from the firmament and advance threateningly upon the earth as if to crush us with its huge and fiery weight.[28]

The second credible account comes from Domingos Coelho, the eye specialist. He reported to the *Ordem* newspaper:

The sun at one moment surrounded with scarlet flame, at another aureoled in yellow and deep purple, seemed to be in an exceedingly fast and whirling movement, at times appearing to be loosened from the sky and to be approaching the earth, strongly radiating heat.[29]

A third witness is Manuel Pedro Marto, also known as Ti-Marto, the father of Jacinta and Francisco, two of the three visionaries. Ti-Marto recounts:

We looked easily at the sun, which for some reason did not blind us. It seemed to flicker on and off, first one way, then another. It cast its rays in many directions and painted everything in different colors— the trees, the people, the air, and the ground. But what was most extraordinary, I thought, was that the sun did not hurt our eyes. Everything was still and quiet, and everyone was looking up. Then at a certain moment, the sun appeared to stop spinning. It then began to move and to dance in the sky until it seemed to detach itself from its place and fall upon us. It was a terrible moment.[30]

Finally, there exist the statements of a journalist from *O Seculo*, which was then Portugal's most important newspaper and was known to be anti-Catholic. The journalist wrote in reference to the sun,

It looked like a plaque of dull silver, and it was possible to look at it without the least discomfort….The sun trembled and made sudden incredible movements outside all cosmic laws.[31]

The extraordinary behavior of the sun that the crowds witnessed on October 13, 1917 can be properly called a miracle. It was beyond the powers of created nature. No created being could have produced such occurrences. The "Miracle of the Sun," as it is now commonly called, confirmed the authenticity of the three children's claims to have seen the Blessed Virgin Mary. The apparitions were officially declared authentic in October of 1930 by Dom Jose Alves Correia da Silva, bishop of the Diocese of Leiria-Fatima.

15. What are the miracles of Lanciano and Siena?

It was around A.D. 700, at the monastery of St. Longinus in Lanciano, Italy, that a priest-monk whose name is unknown witnessed the first, and perhaps the greatest, eucharistic miracle of the Catholic Church. With doubt in his heart about the real presence of Jesus in the Eucharist, the priest prayed the prayer of consecration over the bread and wine. Shortly thereafter, the accidents of bread and wine were transformed into real human flesh and real human blood. The transformed host, which retained the appearance of human flesh, and the blood that coagulated into five globules, still exist today after 1,300 years.

Since 1574, scientific studies have been conducted to examine the miracle. But perhaps the most thorough examination took place under the reign of Pope Paul VI in 1970 by Odoardo Linoli, head physician of the united hospitals of Arezzo, Italy, and Ruggero Bertelli, a professor emeritus of human anatomy at the University of Siena. Their findings, published one year later, showed that the flesh was indubitably muscular tissue from the myocardium of a human heart.[32] To this day the flesh has a pinkish hue, making its blood vessels visible.

The findings of Linoli and Bertelli also show that the blood tested from both the flesh and the coagulated blood was human blood of the AB positive type. Furthermore, the proteins in the coagulated blood were found to have the same percentage ratio found in normal blood. This means the blood had the properties of fresh blood from a living body—it was not extracted from a corpse.

For over 1,300 years the flesh and blood, containing no preservatives, remain in their natural state despite being exposed to various atmospheric and biological agents.[33]

In 1973, the Higher Council of the World Health Organization (WHO) appointed a scientific commission to verify Linoli and Bertelli's findings. After 500 examinations over the course of fifteen months, the commission confirmed all Linoli and Bertelli's conclusions.[34] In 1976 the commission published its research in New York and Geneva.

Another popular eucharistic miracle is the eighteenth-century Miracle of Siena. On August 14, 1730 thieves broke into the Church of San Francesco in Siena, Italy and stole a golden ciborium that contained hundreds of consecrated hosts. After going missing for three days, the sacred hosts were found intact in the alms box of a nearby church, and were immediately taken back in solemn procession to the church of San Francesco.

The hosts had become covered in debris, so they were not consumed but were placed in a tabernacle. Time passed, but the hosts—which, having the accidents of bread, are subject to the physical deterioration that happens to bread over time—did not change in appearance. To their amazement, the priests of the parish found that the hosts not only didn't deteriorate but kept a fresh-baked consistency and a pleasant scent. Official investigations into the authenticity of the miracle would not begin until 1780 (fifty years later) at which time the hosts were still fresh and uncorrupted.

In 1914, Pope St. Pius X ordered a thorough investigation that was conducted by a panel of scientists, professors, theologians, and church leaders. The panel concluded that the hosts "constitute a most unique and interesting phenomenon which reverses the natural laws of conservation of organic matter."[35]

Further examinations were done in 1922, 1950, and 1951. All studies confirmed previous findings. While visiting the city of Siena on September 14, 1980, Pope St. John Paul II said of the hosts, "It is the Real Presence!"[36] After more than 280 years, the sacred hosts still remain in their pristine state to this day.

Both the Miracle of Lanciano and the Miracle of Siena manifest Jesus' desire to arise within us a lively faith in his real presence in the Eucharist. He does not want us to approach the Eucharist as a mere symbol, but as what it truly and substantially is—the body, blood, soul, and divinity of Christ. As he did for the disciples on the road to Emmaus (see Luke 24:31), Jesus is still providing opportunities for his people to have their eyes opened and recognize him in the Eucharist.

16. What are some examples of incorruptible saints?

There have been about a hundred or so incorruptibles in the history of the Church. Let's look at the three that are most famous.

The first is St. Bernadette Soubirous (1844–1879), from Lourdes, France who in 1858, at the age of fourteen, received multiple visits from the Virgin Mary under the title "The Immaculate Conception." This revelation was seen as heavenly confirmation of Pope Pius IX's definition of the dogma four years prior.

Bernadette's body was exhumed on September 22, 1909, thirty years after her death, as part of an official investigation into Bernadette's sanctity. Upon opening the coffin, the two doctors and multiple sisters of the community to which Bernadette belonged, the Sisters of Notre Dame in Nevers, were amazed to find Bernadette's body incorrupt. Her face had a dull white tone with perfectly preserved ears. Her eyebrows, her right eye's eyelashes, and hair were still intact. In contrast to Bernadette's perfectly preserved hands and fingernails, the rosary placed in her hands had rusted and the crucifix that lay upon her chest corroded. The details of the finding were recorded and the tomb was closed up.

Bernadette's corpse was exhumed two more times in the next thirteen years in compliance with standard procedures for the canonization of a saint. Her body was found in basically the same state as it was when she was first exhumed. Her skin did take on a greyish tinge by the third exhumation in 1923 and had patches of mildew, but her body did not putrefy or decompose.

To this day, her body remains visibly incorrupt in a glass reliquary at the Church of St. Gildard in Nevers, France, where she appears to be in a state of restful sleep. The only type of special treatment her body has received is the covering of her face and hands with very fine wax masks in order to disguise the sunken eyes and nose and the blackish tinge on her face and hands.

Pope Pius XI canonized St. Bernadette in 1933. The little town of Lourdes attracts millions of pilgrims from around the world every year seeking both spiritual and physical healings.

Another profound example of an incorruptible is St. Catherine Laboure (1806–1876), who received multiple heavenly visits. The list includes visits from Jesus, St. Vincent de Paul, her guardian angel, and the Blessed Mother, from whom she received the miraculous medal in 1830.

Catherine's corpse was exhumed fifty-six years after her death when the Vatican announced her beatification.

The medical professionals and the ecclesiastical team assigned to the task found her completely intact. Upon first observation, it appeared two fingers on her left hand had blackened due to the corruption of the skin. But upon further investigation the black color turned out to be caused by the disintegration of the sleeve of her habit.

The examination team found her arms and legs to be limber and flexible. They also found her bones to be elastic and cartilaginous. Her intact eyes even retained the blue-gray color she was born with. Her hair did not fall out nor did her fingernails and toenails degrade. Everything was remarkably preserved.

As in Bernadette's case, the preservation of Catherine's body could not be explained by natural causation. It is beyond the powers of created nature and thus is a miracle.

One last example is Bl. Margaret of Castello, the dwarfed Dominican sister who died on April 13, 1320 at thirty-three years of age. The exhumation of Margaret's body was undertaken in 1558 in the presence of a number of official witnesses. To their surprise, Margaret's body looked as though she had just died. Her body was perfectly preserved even though her clothing had crumbled to dust. The physicians involved in the examination affirmed her body was free from all preserving chemicals.

Margaret was beatified on October 19, 1609 and her body can still be seen today under the high altar of the Church of St. Domenico at Citta-di-Castello, Italy. Although there has been a slight discoloration with her skin, and the skin is now dry and a bit hardened, Margaret's body has never been embalmed and is in remarkable condition given it has endured almost 700 years, with the arms supple, eyelashes intact, and nails still present on hands and feet.

The incorruptibles serve as a signpost for the incorruptibility God will give our resurrected bodies in the bodily resurrection at the end of time. As St. Paul writes, "What is sown is perishable, what is raised is imperishable (1 Cor. 15:42).

17. Why doesn't God perform more miracles in order to stop evil and make more people believe in him?

Whenever we hear the question, "Why doesn't God do this or that?" we must always remember that apart from divine revelation we can never know with certainty. As the prophet Isaiah writes, "For my thoughts are not your thoughts, neither are your ways my ways, says the LORD" (Isa. 55:8). Since divine revelation doesn't give any *particular* reasons why God doesn't perform more miracles to stop evil, but only assures that God "works for good with those who love him, who are called according to his purpose" (Rom. 8:28), we can only speculate.

With that understood, we should start by distinguishing between moral evil and physical evil. Moral evil is evil caused by the abuse of human freedom, i.e., sin. Physical evil refers to any sort of suffering, decay, or corruption caused by nature.

Now, when speaking of either kind of evil, it would be wrong to assume God *hasn't* done anything. It may well be that God has already prevented and is preventing horrendous crimes or natural catastrophes that could wipe out the entire human race. There is simply no way, given our spatial and temporal limitations, to know everything he has and hasn't done. As the late philosopher Norris Clarke put it, "Our ignorance cannot be a basis for blaming God for what he is already doing."[37]

If the question concerns physical evil in particular, one possible answer is that an overwhelming presence of miracles might obscure the supernatural character of the miraculous. Consider a scenario where miracles are as common as rain. In such a scenario, it would be difficult (though not impossible) to distinguish between the supernatural and the natural, since we can only know the supernatural by contrast with the natural.

As philosopher Edward Feser points out, such difficulty lends itself to one of two extremes.[38] One extreme is an *occasionalist* view of the world, which holds that God does everything directly without the cooperation of natural causes. The other extreme is the view that there is no order to the universe at all.

This has the potential to lead to an extreme skepticism, or even atheism, since causal regularity is needed to reason to God's existence.

What about moral evil? Why wouldn't God perform more miracles to stop people from committing moral atrocities?

If God were to miraculously stop us from choosing evil, then he would be taking away our capacity for moral choice. But God wills man to have the capacity to choose good *or* evil—at least while we're on earth. God has seen fit to create us in a noble condition where we achieve our eternal reward as a result of our cooperation with him (choosing good over bad) as opposed to giving it to us without our participation (only able to choose good). This being the case, God permits people to choose moral evil.

"But," you may say, "perhaps God doesn't have to take away man's capacity to choose evil, but could just intervene to stop the evil effects of man's bad choices—like changing a fired bullet into butter."

Once again, the answer is that God values the power of moral choice with which he created man. If God never allowed the choices of man to have bad effects, there would be no real value in man's ability to do good or evil. In this case, the alternative of a bad choice would never be a real alternative. Why give humans the capacity to choose evil if there would never be any real effects from that choice?

It's reasonable to conclude, then, that God doesn't ordinarily perform miracles to stop either evil acts or the evil effects caused by them because he values the power of choice he desires man to have.

We can also argue that God permits evil in order to bring about, through a plan beyond our finite comprehension, a greater good. There is no more compelling example of this than Jesus' death on the cross. Had God miraculously stopped the Crucifixion, perhaps we would not have the good of salvation. For sure we would lack knowledge of how far God is willing to go to show us how much he loves us.

These answers by no means fully dispel the darkness of the mystery of why God doesn't perform more miracles to stop evil. However, they do shed a bit of light that may help one navigate the darkness.

18. Why should I pray for a miracle if God is unchangeable and has eternally determined what will happen?

It is true that our prayer requests, including those for miracles, cannot change God's mind. Prayer doesn't move God to say, "Oh, I didn't plan on doing this, but now that Karlo has prayed for it, I'll do it."

We know this is true because God is infinitely perfect. There is no perfection he can acquire or lose, but there would have to be if God could "change his mind." This is why God says in Malachi 3:6, "For I the LORD do not change." But if the Lord can't change, then what is the point of praying for a miracle?

Perhaps we can shed some light on the dilemma by understanding that God's providence involves not only willing certain effects to take place but also the causes from which those effects will be brought about—that is to say, God wills a pattern of cause-effect relationships.

Now, the eternal decree that determines which causes will bring about which effects includes human acts. These actions do not change God's plan, but they are an essential part of it. In the words of Aquinas, "[They] achieve certain effects according to the order of the divine disposition."[39]

Consider an example. God decreed from all eternity that I would have a fried egg for breakfast this morning. However, this eternal decree also involved the egg being produced in the usual way—namely, my wife cracking the egg, putting it into the frying pan, and heating the frying pan on the stove. My wife's actions did not change God's eternal plan but were willed by God to be a part of the cause-effect pattern.

The same is true with prayer, whether it's for a miracle or for something as simple as a beautiful day. Prayer is simply one human action among many (such as my wife cooking the egg) that God wills to be a cause of certain effects in his divine plan.

Prayer doesn't change God's mind but requests

from him that which he has willed from eternity to be bestowed by our prayer. As Brian Davies explains, "God may will from eternity that things should come about as things prayed for by us."[40]

In other words, it is possible that God wills some events to occur only as a result of our prayer. For example, God may have eternally decreed to heal the cancer of a loved one, but only on condition that persistent requests for a miracle are made. Whether we know the effect is conditioned by the request or not doesn't matter. The point is, it's possible, so we make the request hoping that God wills our prayer to be a cause of the effect.

If it turns out he did not will it so, then we trust God has good reasons for his choice. This is why Christians pray, "Thy will be done." We can also take comfort in knowing that God sometimes calls us to pray for our own good. What good might that be? For St. Thomas Aquinas, it's "that we may acquire confidence in having recourse to God and that we may recognize in him the author of our goods."[41]

But if God wills our prayer request to be the cause of the desired effect, it would be true to say our prayer makes a real difference. It would not have made a difference by changing God's mind but by being an essential part of the cause-effect pattern God has eternally decreed.

The real causal power that our prayers have in God's eternal plan is no different from the real causal power my wife's actions had in producing a fried egg this morning. Her actions were essential for the fried egg, because that is how God arranged it to be from all eternity. God has created a world in which fried eggs come to be in a specific way.

Similarly, with regard to prayer, some events will occur only as a result of prayer, because that is the specific way God has arranged it. God has created the world in such a way that our actions, including prayer, serve as real game-changers in the history of the world.

The bottom line is this: there is nothing in the act of prayer that is incompatible with God's changeless and eternal decree. Our petitions, including those for the miraculous, are arranged by God to be part and parcel of his divine plan—a great honor God bestows upon human beings.

19. How do we know God is the cause of an event we say is a miracle? Couldn't it be caused by a demon?

Throughout the centuries Christians have been concerned with how to discern whether an extraordinary event has a divine, angelic, or demonic cause.

With regard to discerning a divine cause, we laid out the criteria in answer 1. Recall the effect must be beyond the power of *created* nature, whether it's in the very essence of the effect produced (e.g., glorification of the body), the subject in which it happens (a corpse receiving life), or the mode or manner in which the effect is produced (immediate healing of a broken bone).

Now, concerning marvelous effects that are not beyond the power of *created* natures but merely beyond powers natural to things (e.g., humans levitating and walking on water), and thus within the realm of angelic and demonic causal influence, the religio-historical context in which the extraordinary event occurs is crucial.

This is the criterion St. Paul used. He writes, "But even if we or an angel from heaven should proclaim to you a gospel contrary to what we proclaimed to you, let that one be accursed!" (Gal. 1:8). The opposite is true as well. If someone performs marvelous deeds in the promotion of the gospel, then we can be sure it is not of demonic origin (see Mark 9:38–39).

Consider the example of Jesus' miracles. They are embedded within the context of his mission to reveal himself and the Father. For example, Jesus believes his exorcisms testify to his making present the Kingdom of God (Matt. 12:28). He heals a paralytic in order that those present would know he has divine authority to forgive sins (Mark 2:9–12). His resurrection, the miracle *par excellence*, vindicates his claims to have power over life and death (John 5:21; 10:17–18). Even those events in Jesus' life that *could* be explained by causal activity of created spirits were in the context of revealing who Jesus was. For example, when Jesus approached the apostles' boat while walking on the sea, he said to the apostles, "Take heart, it is I; have no fear," (Mark 6:51). In the Greek text Jesus used the divine name, "I Am" (*egō eimi*); thus manifesting his divine power.[42]

The same religio-historical context is essential for interpreting marvelous events in Christian history. For example, on the Jewish feast of Pentecost the apostles were able to speak in many different languages (Acts 2:4–12). This is something that doesn't require divine power; it can be brought about by created spirits. But we know this ability was not of demonic origin because the apostles were preaching the resurrection of Jesus and how salvation lies in Jesus alone. It is unlikely that demons would have been empowering the apostles to preach such things about Jesus. As Jesus says, "[I]f Satan casts out Satan, he is divided against himself; how then will his kingdom stand?" (Matt. 12:26).

The apostles experienced many other wondrous events that could be explained by created spirits—e.g., causing the building to shake by their preaching (Acts 4:31) and having prison cell doors open by themselves (Acts 5:17–25; 12:5–11; 16:25–30)—but all these events were ordered to the promotion of the Christian message. Once again, it doesn't make sense for demons to help the apostles preach the message they were opposed to.

The same is true for Christian miracles and marvelous deeds throughout the centuries—especially in the lives of the saints. The saints of the Church have performed both miracles and marvelous deeds. Those occurrences that are beyond the powers of created natures are sure to have God as their cause. With regard to marvelous deeds, it is the performance of them *in the name of Jesus* and within the context of promoting the Christian message that precludes demonic activity.

Discerning the nature of extraordinary events and the cause behind them is not an easy task. It can be tricky. But this is why Jesus gave us the Catholic Church guided by the Holy Spirit. As long as we stay close to the Church, we can avoid being "[T]ossed to and fro and blown about by every wind of doctrine, by people's trickery, [and] by their craftiness in deceitful scheming" (Eph. 4:14).

20. How should Catholics approach claims to the miraculous?

A Catholic should first of all approach miraculous claims with a healthy skepticism. We don't want to be gullible, believing every miraculous claim. To believe every message that purports to come from God without sufficient evidence constitutes a sin of imprudence.

It is important that we approach alleged miracles with a critical eye, which is the approach of the Church. Following the instruction of St. Paul to test all things

(1 Thess. 5:21), the Church often invites unbelieving scientists to be members of the teams employed to officially investigate miracle claims. The Church wants to rule out all natural and preternatural explanations before it accepts an event as miraculous. In other words, it separates the wheat from the chaff (Luke 3:17). If a healthy skepticism is the Church's approach to the miraculous, then it should be ours too.

Now, while we don't want to be gullible we also don't want to become so skeptical that we *never* believe in any miracles. This constitutes a second element of the Catholic approach. As we've seen, there are numerous miracles approved by the Church that can be used to strengthen the faith of believers and lead unbelievers to faith. It would be offensive to God to ignore such generous gifts and never use them for evangelization.

A third aspect of the Catholic approach is that we don't want to be miracle-chasers, trying to see God's miraculous power in everything (e.g., I see Mary's face in a potato chip). Jesus had some harsh words for those people for whom miracles had become like an addiction. When asked what sign he would give, Jesus responded, "An evil and adulterous generation seeks for a sign" (Matt. 12:39).

Perhaps the reason for Jesus' terseness is that the constant need for a miracle signifies a lack of faith. Jesus wants us to be content with the one sign he promised to give, namely his death and resurrection (Matt.

12:39–40). His resurrection should be sufficient for moving us to faith.

A fourth point to consider is that a Catholic needs to always keep in mind the true purpose of miracles. Often people seek signs simply to be wowed or entertained, and thus forget that miracles are meant to glorify God and lead people to salvation. God doesn't want people to focus so much on the gift that they lose sight of the gift-giver.

Finally, a fifth element of the Catholic approach to the miraculous is submission to the judgment of the Church. The Church has been given by Christ to guide and lead us by the Holy Spirit. As Catholics, we should look to the Church as our mother who watches over us and keeps us from going astray.

According to Jesus, we don't have to go chasing after miracles because the miracles will chase after us (Mark 16:17). The Church is Christ's body here on earth and his Spirit animates it. As such, there will always be miracles. It is important that we as Christians use these miracles not only to strengthen our own faith but also to show unbelievers the reality of God and the truth of his revelation through his Son, Jesus Christ.

About the Author

Karlo Broussard is a staff apologist and speaker for Catholic Answers. He holds undergraduate and graduate degrees in theology from Catholic Distance University and the Augustine Institute, and is currently working on his masters in philosophy with Holy Apostles College and Seminary.

Endnotes

1 First Vatican Council, *The Dogmatic Constitution on the Catholic Faith*, Ch. 3; emphasis added.

2 See David Hume, *An Enquiry Concerning Human Understanding*, Section X.

3 C.S. Lewis, *Miracles* (New York: Harper Collins), 74–75, Kindle edition.

4 See Edward J. Thomas, *The Life of Buddha as Legend and History* (London: Routledge and Kegan Paul, 1949), 211–248.

5 See William Lane Craig, *The Son Rises: The Historical Evidence for the Resurrection of Jesus* (Eugene: Wipf and Stock Publishers, 1981).

6 The atheist activist and historian Richard Carrier, in chapter 11 of his book *Not the Impossible Faith*, objects to this appeal to women. For his arguments and responses to them, see Karlo Broussard, "Why the Resurrection Was Not a Conspiracy," catholic.com.

7 *Catechism of the Catholic Church*, par. 337, 362, 396,

8 First Vatican Council. *Dogmatic Constitution of the Catholic Faith*, Ch. II.

9 Pope Pius XII, *Divino Afflante Spiritu,* sec. 38.

10 See E.C. Messenger, "The Miraculous Element in the Bible," in *A Catholic Commentary on Holy Scripture* ed. by Dom Bernard Orchard, O.S.B., (New York: Thomas Nelson and Sons, 1953).

11 The *Catechism of the Catholic Church*, in paragraph 2580, makes this point when it explains how King Solomon, when dedicating the Temple in 1 Kings 8, appeals to the miracles of the Exodus as part and parcel of Israel's foundation as God's covenantal people.

12 For the historical reliability of the Old Testament miracles, see K.A. Kitchen, *The Reliability of the Old Testament* (Grand Rapids:

Eerdmans, 2006). For the historical reliability of the New Testament miracles, see John P. Meier, *A Marginal Jew: Rethinking the Historical Jesus*, Vol. 2. *Mentor, Message, and Miracles* (New York: Doubleday, 1994).

13 See E.C. Messenger, 119.

14 For an in-depth study see John P. Meier 1994, *A Marginal Jew: Rethinking the Historical Jesus*, Vol. 2 (New York: Doubleday), Chapters 17–23.

15 This argument was so effective among the Jews that it was used hundreds of years later in the Talmud. For example, Kallah 1b claims Mary herself admitted that on the day of her wedding Joseph left her and an evil spirit lay with her in order to conceive Jesus. Thus, it was believed Jesus had a literal demon as his father.

16 See Graham H. Twelftree, *Jesus the Exorcist* (Peabody: Hendrickson, 1991). See also Graham Twelftree, *Jesus the Miracle Worker* (Downers Grove: InterVarsity Press, 1999).

17 See Raymond Brown 1994, *An Introduction to New Testament Christology* (New York: Paulist Press), 63.

18 The term glorious here refers to the unique powers of Jesus' resurrected body, such as freedom from the limitations of space (see John 20:19) and the ability to appear and disappear (see Luke 24:31). For a study on the glorious nature of Jesus' resurrected body, see Robert J. Spitzer, *God So Loved the World: Clues to Our Transcendent Destiny from the Revelation of Jesus* (San Francisco: Ignatius Press, 2016), ch. 4.

19 CCC 643 – "Christ's Resurrection cannot be interpreted as something outside the physical order, and it is impossible not to acknowledge it as an historical fact."

20 See Flavius Josephus, *Antiquities of the Jews*, 4.8.15.

21 See N.T. Wright, *The Resurrection of the Son of God* (Minneapolis: Fortress Press, 2003), 205.

22 Ibid.

23 Ibid., 273.

24 Ibid., 78–82.

25 Charles Mortimer Carty, *Padre Pio—The Stigmatist* (Tan Books, 1973), 158

26 Ibid.

27 Ibid.

28 John de Marchi, *The True Story of Fatima* (Irondale: EWTN), https://www.ewtn.com/library/MARY/tsfatima.htm.

29 Ibid.

30 Ibid.

31 Ibid.

32 Zenit, "Physician Tells of Eucharistic Miracle of Lanciano," https://zenit.org/articles/physician-tells-of-eucharistic-miracle-of-lanciano/

33 See Joan Carroll Cruz, *Eucharistic Miracles* (Charlotte: Tan Books, 1986), 3–7.

34 See "Physician Tells of Eucharistic Miracle of Lanciano" at https://zenit.org/articles/physician-tells-of-eucharistic-miracle-of-lanciano/

35 Real Presence Eucharistic Education and Adoration Association, "Eucharistic Miracle of Siena," http://www.therealpresence.org/eucharst/mir/english_pdf/Siena.pdf

36 Ibid.

37 W. Norris Clarke, *The One and the Many: A Contemporary Thomistic Metaphysics* (Indiana: Notre Dame Press, 2001), 288.

38 Edward Feser, "God, Reason, & Reality: Symposium with Ed Feser,

Anselm Ramelow, OP & Michael Dodds, OP," https://www.you-tube.com/watch?v=e-KDAXaP_3E.

39 St. Thomas Aquinas, *Summa Theologiae*, II–II:83:2.

40 Brian Davies, *Thinking About God* (Eugene: Wipf & Stock, 2010), 319.

41 *Summa Theologiae*, II–II:83:2

42 The Greek text for the expression, "It is I," reads *egō eimi*, which literally translates "I Am." This is the name that is often used in the Old Testament for God (see Exod. 3:14; Deut. 32:39). Although *egō eimi* can be used simply to identify oneself (see Mark 13:6), the context suggests a divine usage. For reasons why the expression should be taken in its divine sense, see Brant Pitre, *The Case for Jesus* (New York: Image, 2016), 127–131.

Become part of the team.
Help support Catholic Answers.

Catholic Answers is an apostolate dedicated to serving Christ by bringing the fullness of Catholic truth to the world. We help good Catholics become better Catholics, bring former Catholics "home," and lead non-Catholics into the fullness of the Faith.

Catholic Answers neither asks for nor receives financial support from any diocese. The majority of its annual income is in the form of donations from individual supporters like you.

To make a donation by phone using your credit card, please speak with one of our customer service representatives at 888-291-8000.

To make a donation by check, please send a check payable to "Catholic Answers" to:

> Catholic Answers
> 2020 Gillespie Way
> El Cajon, CA 92020

To make a donation online, visit **catholic.com**.

TO EXPLAIN & DEFEND THE FAITH

catholic.com